four sweet seasons

ASHLIN VESELKA

Design: Martin Farrell

ISBN: 0692921230
ISBN-13: 978-0692921234

to the one who broke my heart,
thank you for giving me these words
to tell this sweet story to bring God all the glory.

t a b l e   o f   c o n t e n t s

i n t r o

I don't know what made you pick up this book, but I'm glad you're here because if anything I want you to know that you're never alone in the middle of your pain. It's not something that you should ever run from. These pages drip with messy heart thoughts, all in hopes to encourage you to run straight into it. Run heart first into the pain so that Jesus can heal you, it's the only real way to do it. Truth is, I learned what love is by experiencing, for far too long, everything that it is not. It was one of my biggest blessings, but also my heaviest burdens.

We have all gone through seasons of heartbreak and healing, of ruin and redemption, of sadness and surrender. It's not always easy to talk about, the raw thoughts and feelings that come with the pain, so I just hope that these poems help you journey through whatever season you're in. I hope it encourages your heart to start voicing your hurt even if it feels impossibly hard and ridiculously scary.
This is a story based on true events, it's divided into four chapters, starting in the Fall - each one representing the seasons as the story quite literally unfolded similarly in real life.
I pray that it helps you to make the choice to run from the one who broke you and walk straight into the loving arms of the One who really wants to be with you,

w o u l d   y o u   w a l k   w i t h   m e ?

fall.

f a l l i n g   a p a r t .

the season where it starts to crumble

I feel like I'm going to stumble

piece by piece

ache to ache

pain and even more pain

I don't know where it started

but I'm here and I can barely breathe

I never thought I'd have to leave

I thought you'd always choose me

but you've stopped and now I'm falling apart

where did I go wrong?

why does it feel so good to cry?

that's not normal

but it feels normal

it's the only way I know how to breathe

I keep holding on

but I know we're falling apart

I feel it start

the break begins to crack open my heart

e s c a p i n g .

everyday I try picking up the pieces

but it's all too heavy to hold

I'm too weak to do it on my own

you look at the pieces of my heart on the floor

and begin to act like I'm some sort of chore

I put in the effort, but you rarely do

truth is, you only want my body these days

when you need a break from all the haze

like I'm some sort of escape from

the madness inside your head

but as soon as you get high again

every part of you gets cold

isn't this getting old?

I don't even know who you are anymore

it hurts to even look at you

I can't figure out what I'm supposed to do

you've lost your way

don't I even get a say?

you've made this mess

you only care about the success

I only care about your best

I know this is not the way it's suppose to be

I don't feel free

I don't feel like me

too bad no one can hear me

black hole.

he uses you, he abuses you

it's both the mental

and physical games he plays

you don't want to be touched like that

but you let him because it makes you feel

like he still loves you

it's past midnight and he crawls into bed

you know the game he's about to play with your head

he pulls you into the black hole

you can't see and it feels like you've lost your soul

what are you doing there?

you were not created for a life in the dark

you were made for the light

get out, leave

you were made for so much more

stop leaving pieces of yourself on his bedroom floor

p a i n   e r a s e r .

no one knows

I feel empty and I can't help but feel so alone

I don't know where to go

I hide what's really going on inside

I drink straight from the bottle to ease the pain

I try to get it down quick

just so I can tolerate being around you

without getting sick

my head feels numb

I don't want morning to come

it's the only way I know how to be these days

when you're high and I'm sober

it reminds my heart that it really is over

and I just don't want that to be true

at least not tonight

I have no strength in me to put up a fight

b e t t e r   w e e k e n d s .

please realize that there's a better life

one that doesn't include numbing yourself

to ease the pain he's caused

you deserve a Friday filled with fun

you deserve a Saturday spent in the sun

you deserve a Sunday soaked in peace

you won't get that here with him

he doesn't care about your feelings

he's made that loud and clear

just because he makes you feel wanted when he's high

it doesn't mean his heart is near

there's a life full of freedom

waiting on the other side

what are you waiting for?

<u>t h e   p l a n t   y o u   w a t e r .</u>

you've chosen the plant,

all while I'm still believing

there's a possibility you'll change.

r e d   h u e s .

the leaves on the trees

have changed to a violent red

we're driving in your car

and not a word is being said

it's dark and it's late

you have a breakdown

I can't remember the date

but as I sit in the passenger seat

I can tell you feel like those demons got you beat

it's the first time I've seen you this way in six years

it's clear now, I'm seeing all the things you truly fear

it's pouring out of you

you speed down the street

you're losing control

you feel broken deep down in your soul

you've been too high

for way too long

you don't know how to stop

you don't know how to be without it anymore

the guy you are when you're high is an illusion

the smoke gives you that kind of confusion

when you're sober it hurts too much

you shout in anger

you shout in pain

you get out of the car

you feel like you're going insane

I run after you

with tears pouring down my face

your voice gets louder

you keep telling me to leave this place

I see your broken heart

and I don't know what to do

because after all, mines broken too

it was that night that I realized

I'd never be the one to fix you

with demons so real and

a heart so far from where you've been

God would be the only one able to find you again

t r u s t   m e ,   h e   w o n ' t .

he wasn't always this way

that's why you continue to stay

you've seen the good

so your heart can't just leave

even though you know you should

it's hard because you've seen the other side

so you think he'll change back with time

you tell yourself that by staying,

he will see you're worth being better for

but here's the thing

he really won't

he knows full well that you deserve more

but he also knows that you've loved him

better than anyone else ever has before

so he'll do just enough to keep you holding on

but he's too far gone, he really won't change for you

trust me, he just won't.

w h a t   l o v e   i s   n o t .

confusing.

misleading.

forceful.

compromising.

selfish.

conditional.

wavering.

impatient.

self seeking.

mean.

deceiving.

one-sided.

grey.

s i l l y   m e .

every day I wonder where the guy

that I fell in love with went

and I begin to realize his time has gone,

he's been spent

four years was all we really had

and for the last two

let's just be real, we both knew

satan got a hold of your heart

and no matter how hard I try

I can't pull you two apart

I've tried and I've tried

if you only knew the amount of tears I've cried

I've used up all of the strength inside me

to pull apart the grip he has on your heart

silly me, I was wrong

to think that I could break something so strong

g o , g e t o u t .

you can't change him

so stop trying

get out

before you lose more of you than you already have

there's no use in fighting for someone

who doesn't fight for you

there's no use in staying with someone

who takes you for granted

i w o n d e r .

I want the old you to come back

I hope you still might genuinely care

but you treat me like I'm just not there

you're the guy I could have loved for a lifetime

I wonder where along the way you lost yourself

it's like you put me up on a shelf

like you're saving me for later

but what about right now?

how do expect us to last?

your only concern is making money and fast

what made you stop loving me?

how did we even end up here?

I feel so unwanted

I feel used

I never thought I'd feel so abused

I need out, but I feel too weak to even speak

what love shouldn't make you feel.

unworthy.

used.

worthless.

dirty.

abused.

trapped.

helpless.

not enough.

too much.

weak.

small.

scared.

insecure.

doubtful.

worried.

s h e l f   l o v e .

don't let him make a shelf love out of you.

p l a y i n g   p r e t e n d .

I start to do this twisted thing
where I paint a picture of who you could be
I maintain that imagine in my mind
and I push everything else to the side
it's all I choose to see
it's the only thing that brings me comfort,
hanging onto this make believe version
of you and me.

b a i t .

you say you're too busy

you claim to have put in your time with me

you expect me to wait

like I'm some kind of bait

I get angry, I get mad, but yet I stay

I have nothing, yet everything left to say

d e v i l   l e v e l .

he's dancing with the devil
can't you see?
it's clear that he won't ever be able to love you,
playing around on that level

s h o w e r   t e a r s .

I keep my mouth shut most days
while you continue to say this is just a phase
so why does it feel like you've been saying that
for the majority of these days?
I never know when you're in a good mood
I continue not knowing what to do
it's not how it's supposed to be
the crying in the shower so no one sees
the constant one-way conversations
I have in my head
all over a relationship that for too long
has been dead
trying to convince my heart of something
that it already knows is true
I fight it day in and day out,
all while knowing what I already knew
it's draining, I'm exhausted – but I can't let go
when is enough, enough and how will I know?

u n g l u e d .

don't stay with the man who tries to keep you small
just so he can feel big
he makes you think that you need him to survive,
but his need to keep you small is only because
he sees your potential
he sees how amazing you really could be
and that scares him
because if you start to see it too,
then maybe you'd realize what he already knew
that maybe you really are going to something in this
world and the idea of that makes him come unglued

d e a d   d r e a m s .

we've been together so long

we invested so much here

I grew roots without fear

I planted dreams with you

but now I'm just living with you in your sin

you use to be everything I dreamed of

maybe if I could remind you again

yet you're so different now

you're lost in the clouds

will you ever come down?

things don't ever seem like they'll be the same

I wonder where it changed

where I went wrong

where is God anyway?

I thought He had my back

maybe it's just my communication

with Him that lacks

character calling.

you fell in love as kids

of course you'll both change

you became a Godly woman along the way

you're strong

you're secure

you're loyal

you're not afraid

you're honest

you're real

you're capable

you're determined

you're able to see what matters in life

you're not afraid to call him out

to refine his character

but he doesn't want to hear it

he doesn't want to be confronted

he doesn't think he'll ever get caught

he doesn't like the woman you've become

because now you start calling out his flaws

and he doesn't like to be told what to do

he's the type of man who needs control

only because he's lost himself

so if he can control you

then at least he has his grip on something

but he doesn't know how to love you anymore

because he doesn't know how to love himself

he hears you, he knows your right

but he doesn't change because you've stayed this long,

he doesn't think you're going anywhere

a simple request.

you're just asking to be loved

but he's addicted to the drug

it's made him forget how to feel

you must know that you're not asking for a lot,

you're just asking him to be everything he is not

empty miles.

I continue to fall deeper into this mess

I feel it, I'm getting further away from my best

I keep numbing the pain

all while you stay the same

manipulating me with your mental games

you just keep getting higher

and it's making you the very best liar

it hurts me so much

the higher you get

the further I fall

I don't know what to believe anymore

I sit beside you and my heart feels empty

it's like you're a million miles away

you rarely have anything loving to say

you make it so hard to breathe

I have to watch what I say

the name of Jesus is like word vomit to you these days

I ignore it because I'm scared

that you just might walk away

I can't leave now

there's nothing better out there for me

the money is flowing

you convince me that

you're just in the process of growing

you say it won't always be this way

so I stay, I always stay

n o t h i s B a r b i e .

you treat me like your Barbie doll

you act like you purchased me at a price

you put me in my box on a Sunday

then you tell me you're busy working

till next Monday

and you expect me to stand there

with the perfect hair

then you go out in the middle of the week

please tell me how is that fair?

you claim that it's for work

you say you weren't there long

funny, how you always say you didn't stay

for more than two songs

like two is somehow the magic number

that won't get you caught

but you should know better

I was never a woman who could be bought

you put it all up to making the connections

but all you really cared about was

getting into the VIP section

Saturday rolls around

you're working downtown

it's clear, you only want to play with your doll

so you give me a call

and as soon as you get what you need

you say you have to go back to work

it's almost eleven

and just like that

you're done with your little slice of heaven

t h e   o n l y   c h o i c e .

you keep saying you're too busy
so why do I stay with someone
who doesn't make time to actually be with me?
where is the love in that?
why can't I just walk away?

I care too much
my heart isn't like yours
you won't ever understand
but I have to go
I have no other choice
I need to use my voice

s m o k e   s u r g e s .

we rarely talk about the future anymore,

but when we do, I just keep telling you

that I won't have a drawer filled with that drug

you say it wouldn't ever be that way

but yet it already is

and instead of a drawer

you choose an entire room

it's where satan now easily looms

you inhale on the daily to reach your high

the smoke surges through your bloodstream

and just like that, you turn into a different guy

it's not the one I know

he's been gone for awhile

I can barely breathe

I hate this

it's killing our dreams

we're falling apart at the seams

w h a t   s c a r e s   m e   m o r e .

the money has your heart

it's what keeps tearing us apart

all you want is more

and now, to you, I'm just a bore

why would I stay with a man whose heart

is attached to all of the green?

can't you see that you're destroying me

like one of those awful break up scenes?

I know I deserve better

way more than I've been settling for

yet I remain in this place

I can't figure out what scares me more

me walking away

or you leaving me?

I don't want what you have to offer me

it's nothing but pain

why am I staying when there's no life to gain?

the difference.

he throws his money at the problem,
while she throws her feelings
that's the difference.

c a t + m o u s e .

falling apart piece by piece

it hurts so much

yet I think I can still fix it on my own

I cover it up with

with my substance of choice

as if no one will ever know

I try to hold it all together

I keep putting in the effort

but you keep talking down to me

you make me feel so small

why do you always forget to call?

you're always late

you never want to go out on dates

you have to get high every time we leave your house

I feel like we're playing this

sick game of cat and mouse

I'm falling apart in front of your eyes

I'm beginning to see now

that all of it was pure lies

why am I staying?

you tell me to leave if I'm so unhappy here

you push me to walk away

you've been playing these games for quite a while

you treat like I'm some kind of child

who is supposed to mind

I want to leave so bad

yet I want to stay too

I never wanted to be the girl

who walked away from you

#askingforafriend.

why do introverts

think that they

can love the demons

out of the extroverts?

i t   c o s t s   t o o   m u c h .

walking away from a toxic place

doesn't make you weak

it makes you strong

and you're so much stronger than you think

stop calling that place home

you were not meant to play games

he's destroying your peace of mind

he's cost you so much already

you feel broke

of all your emotions

you have nothing else to give

you keep pulling on every string

and it's unraveling

you deserve something

that doesn't come undone so easily

smoke jokes.

you don't know your left from your right

the money and the fame cover up the real fight

the one going on inside of your heart every night

it was almost too clear from the start

you're heart deep in the business

you hurt me more than you'll ever admit

so now you cope with all of the stress

by just staying lit

to cover up the pain

and bury the madness going on inside of your brain

you really can't see it?

you're tearing me apart

with every single inhale

you're getting further away from my heart

I think that's what hurts the most

is that you'd rather have the smoke

and treat me like some sort of joke

it's not fair

I hate seeing you this way

I just want the old you back

the one whose head was clear

who made me feel like no matter what

I had nothing to fear

a   w e e k e n d   a f f a i r .

I've given you everything and more

yet you continue to leave us

in pieces on the floor

I don't know how to do it anymore

it's clear now that you no longer care

I'm nothing more than a weekend affair

I only sound good to you when you have the time

but you always have to work

so you say I can come over

but it's no surprise, you're as high as a kite

then you stare into your computer

for the rest of the night

no wonder every time we speak

there's a fight

you say I don't see the vision

you say I just don't get it

the problem is you only see

what you want to when you're lit

s a n d c a s t l e   k i n g .

I'm trying to understand

what's so great about building your life on the sand?

you know it doesn't last, so what's the point?

I guess I'll be back next weekend because truth is

I will always be your number one fan

a b o u t   t i m e .

why do I keep going back to that toxic place you live?

I deserve more

I deserve better

I say I'll do it later

but I know it's about time

that I get back home to my Creator

b i r t h d a y h a z e .

I turn 24 today

I'm the furthest thing from okay

you take me to a show

an artist I barely even know

you put me in the back of your car

you take me along for the ride

as I watch you get high with all the guys

my heart gets so heavy

I can't breathe

why do I want to get high too?

I guess to escape this feeling

but that would make me like you

and that's the last thing I want to do

I wish you'd hold my hand

why can't for one second

you act like you're my man?

we listen to these songs

the music is loud

there are so many people around

I can't even hear myself think

I feel the tension build in you

I'm afraid to even make a sound

I stay quiet as I always do

I get another drink to numb

the pain swirling in my brain

how many is that now?

I lost count

I get tired and I need to sit

it's no surprise, you leave me for the VIP

and just like that, you lose sight of me

I'm so much better than this

these people are so lost

is this life really worth that cost?

I hang my head heavy between my knees

and hear the Holy Spirit speak

it's nothing, but a mere whisper -

'you don't belong here, My Dear'

I'm sitting on the ground

I'm drunk, but my soul is sober

and just like that, I know that it's over

b r e a k i n g   t o   h e a l .

I've lost myself in loving you

you're always pressuring me to get high,

like I'm just one of the guys

don't you remember my heart is sick?

I know there's so much more to life

I can see so clearly now

I have to say goodbye

I know I have to go, but how?

that question settles into a place of my heart

that I can't ignore anymore

I don't even know where to start

I've had enough

I must to go

it's clear what I already know

the time has come, I'm ready to go

I feel so weak

but God's so much stronger than I think

taking the step

making the call

it's all I need to do

before I really fall

I'm doing this for me

first I'll break

but then I'll heal

it's going to be a long process

I feel like I already know the deal

winter.

p a c k i n g   b a g s .

yesterday I turned 24

and my head feels like I just spent hours

banging it against the floor

I wake up next to you feeling so used

my mind and my body, torn apart and abused

what even happened last night?

I'm so confused

I never thought in a million years

you'd be the one to live this kind of life

it's 6 am and I can't sleep

I keep asking God why you don't see me

as valuable enough to keep

I lie awake next to you

as you breathe so easily next to me

as if you did nothing wrong

like we're fine

why can't you be the one to leave

you're just waiting for me to walk away right?

you want me to be the one who gives up?

I guess you win

today is the day I stop giving into you and your sin

yet I'd still give anything to be able to stay

I pack my bags as you sleep

you don't even realize

that I can barely keep it together

you wake up and ask me what's wrong

as if last night didn't happen

you act like we're fine

you hold the money above my head

twisting my mind

but we're not okay

you test me

seeing how long it'll take till I break

I say nothing is wrong

I'm always doing that and

I say it for the very last time

I can't find the words to speak

I grab my bag and leave before I become too weak

n o   b u t   y e s   b u t   n o .

too many times you said no with a shrug

you felt weak

then you said no with a shove

you begin to feel sick

you said it again

that time with a shove deep into his ribs

he didn't care

he was high

and you were sober enough to know

that you didn't want to

but you lie there in the dark

and the tension fills the air

you think if you don't say yes he'll leave you

so you give in

you let him have every part of you

you feel used, but you don't know what else to do

you know in your head it's not right

you know in your heart you want to put up a fight

but you tell yourself it's okay

if it's just for one more night

you don't stop it because even if

it's not how you want to be loved

you feel loved for the briefest moment

and that's enough for now

you know in the morning it won't be this way

his touch won't feel the same

so you keep giving in

because even if it's just for the night

it's better than nothing

it's better than risking him leaving

but it's not

don't mistake his lust for love, open your eyes

he doesn't know how to love you when he's sober

he doesn't know how to love you when he's high

he doesn't know who he is at all

so he doesn't know how to love you

he's so lost, don't lose yourself too

God's got something so much better for you

w h i t e   m a r b l e   f l o o r s .

I get home and collapse on the bathroom floor

the weight of my heart is too heavy to hold

the tears pour out yet again

and here I am, still living with you in your sin

I can barely catch my breath

I press the side of my face into

the cold white marble floor

praying that the temperature will hit my core and

stop my heart from bleeding even more

it hurts, it aches

my insides feel like they are literally going to break

I don't hear from you all morning

you must be downtown

it's sad how much that money's got your soul bound

why do I feel so much?

I just want to throw up

I find my way to stand on my feet

I look into the mirror and feel so broken

I start to weep

I don't even know the girl looking back at me

does God see what I see?

I pray for the words to speak

it's only been a few hours and I feel so weak

my mind knows the things I must say

and yet my heart wishes

I didn't have to walk away

I ask God if there's any other way

but it's been a minute since we've talked

I know He hasn't left me

but I feel so distant from His voice

I get it, it was always my choice

but I'm here now and I need Jesus more than

I need the air in my lungs

I know I heard Him last night

I realize now, His voice remains the same

even on the darkest nights

I feel like I can't breathe

I think back to how you made me feel

and easily send a text to seal the deal

y o u r   d a y   o n e .

I tell you I have to go

you try telling me I just don't know

I say you're just pretending to be someone you're not,

but you'd never admit to being caught

you're too concerned in making your name known

you never have the time to even pick up the phone

I'm slipping from your fingertips with each text sent

you see me pouring my heart out

and yet you don't do a thing about it

you read through it as if I'm not serious

you tell me that I'm emotionally all over the place

but that's really just an excuse for you to use

truth is, you've never been okay with a woman

who pushes you to conquer what you truly fear

no one but me and your Creator know

the real demons that you face

don't you remember that night in your car,

down the street from your place?

I can see it and He does too

you simply feel like you're too far gone

you're entangled in the debt

you're attached to the green

you're caught up in that scene

I'm no longer the love you think you need

I've been there since day one

before all the money came

remember when our dreams use to be the same?

I gave you my loyalty from the very start

yet now you keep giving yours over to the things

that inside are just tearing you apart

I guess I'll never understand

you're just not the same

you know you're living in sin

but you don't want to put up a real fight

you claim to do it for the big picture

you say you're only playing the part

yet you can't see that in doing so

you have completely destroyed us

t h e   l o v e   y o u   n e e d .

he's no longer playing the part

he's the part and he's got you playing

your heart is too good

to be caught up in his mess

stop playing his games

walk away and get back to your best

let Jesus love you for real

you don't even know what that feels like

go get that love, it's the one you've always needed

s t a y g o n e .

if he chooses it over you

let him, don't beg him

you're worth so much more than that

his choices make up what's in his heart

it doesn't define who you are

you're worthy of the choice

he may have made you feel worthless

but one day, he'll come to the end of himself

and then what will he have left?

not you because you'll be long gone by then

don't worry, he'll regret choosing his sin

please don't go back

you're so much better off without him

m a s k   r e f l e c t i o n s .

it's no longer a mask

it has become who he really is

there's no taking it off anymore

it reflects everything that he stands for

that's what happens when you start toying

with different faces

eventually life will make you choose

he just picked the one where he gained

the whole world

and lost you

s i l e n t   w a r s .

it's been days

the silence between us is killing my heart

I ask for a face to face

truth is, I knew it was over

but after six years who wouldn't need a goodbye?

I knew I had to stop believing satan's lies

you lost me so long ago

you're so far away

you're beyond my reach

you don't realize what you've lost

what letting me go is really going to cost

you probably won't for quite some time

only because that green has you thinking

that you're doing better than fine

t h e   r e d   r o o m .

we sit in this familiar room

it's illuminated with red lights

I've been here before, one too many nights

the music is loud

the smoke is heavy

I have so much to say

but I don't know where to start

I guess I just want to know

when did it start falling apart?

I try to tell you how I feel

but as I look into your eyes

I begin to wonder, why do I even try?

you're too high to even see me straight

it's dark out and it's getting late

I feel frozen from the inside out

will I ever have the right words?

I say everything that I can

but it feels like I'm drowning

your eyes are glazed over

your heart is cold

for the first time in my life

I have no more words to say

I know I have to be bold

walking away is my only choice

my mouth runs dry, trying to find my voice

you stare at me blankly

claiming how you've been living is fine

I knew for far too long

you had already crossed the line

the smoke filled your bloodstream

it made a home in your heart

it clouded your ability to see that what we had

you easily let fall apart

I don't want things this way

I just want you to want me to stay

I want to be wanted

I want to be loved

I want to be touched in a way that makes me feel safe

I want to see your face and feel a warm embrace

I want you to stop being someone you're not

yet you push me away

instead of owning up to being caught

you tell me to stop talking so loud

you're afraid of what other people may think

who cares?

they're just downstairs

pouring more drinks

and I sit there with my heart in your hands

but it's in so much pain

it's like you squeezed the life out of it

I no longer think I can sit

I get up to leave

I think by now I've had enough

I realize there's not going to be a goodbye

you're too far gone

you're sold out to the money

all you care about is that dream killing honey

as I open the door to walk away

your hand comes out of no where

like you're trying to force me to stay

it takes everything in me not to turn around

and forget about the last few days

but with the strength I have left, I open the door

the cold winter air hits me and it's a shock to my body

from the outside in, I feel free

free from the smoke, free from the games

free from the torment you put on my brain

I get in my car without looking back

I sit there for a minute, thinking you'd come after me

I don't want to believe

that you'd let me leave like this

I never could make you choose me

and I couldn't force myself to stay for one more day

so I start my car and drive away

my tears cloud my vision

my heart feels as if you just made the biggest incision

you broke me in a million pieces that night

and the saddest part is

you didn't even do one thing to put up a fight

f r e s h   p a i n .

the day after the day I left

it's no surprise I have so much pain in my chest

the real kind that comes with having a heart too big

that's what I think you forget all the time

I have a heart of a different kind

but you don't care about that anymore

remember when you use to?

I wake up feeling sick

I want to throw up

I want to give up

I want to go Home

I know God's here

I know He's got me and there's nothing to fear

yet somehow I feel like all of me is too broken

I can't hear myself think

I feel like I need a drink

but I don't want to be like you

using some sort of substance

to hide my pain in sin

I won't ever do that to me and my heart again

I have no idea where I'm suppose to go from here

I've feared this place for so long

yet I knew it was coming

I knew I had to go, I knew it for months

and now I'm here

I shouldn't have anything to fear

God's with me now, but I feel so alone

I feel broken

I can't get out of bed, not today

it's too fresh, the pain is too real

how can this really be the end?

I know it's the end

I know it's over

it hurts so much more when I'm sober

I hate that it's this way

what I would give to do it over again

why didn't you come after me last night?

I thought I was what you wanted

I feel worthless, I feel used, I feel replaceable

I feel empty

I feel too broken to even move

I don't want to do anything

but I know I need to seek God's face

it's all I can do to get me through this place

this pain is too much to bear

I don't want the sun to be up

I want the night

I want the dark

I don't want to see the light

I want to sleep till the pain is gone

I don't want to open my eyes

because I know when I do

I'll see that everything was just disguised as a lie

I just want to sleep

can't I just sleep?

I don't want to eat

I feel like I can't even stand on my own two feet

I feel weak

I feel small

I feel fragile

why do I just want you to call?

s o m u c h m o r e .

if he doesn't choose you,

let him lose you

you deserve so much more

than you've been settling for

w i n t e r   l i e s .

weeks have passed
the leaves on the trees have fallen
the branches are bare
they look frail and weak
I feel like God's telling me
that I'm the same right now

I can barely speak
you so easily let our relationship die
you left me stuck here this winter
without any kind of goodbye

letters you don't get to read.

everyday I get better
but why do I keep writing you letters?
maybe I'm hoping that you'd come back
too bad I already know the facts
you don't love me like you love the honey
I want to reach out
I want to hear your voice again
how long has it been?
the winter is passing
and it feels like I've been fasting

t o x i c   l o v e .

he pushed you to walk away
so it makes it look like you were the one to give up
well you did,
on a toxic love
that you didn't even realize was making you sick
don't ever feel like you gave up on him
he gave up on you long before you walked away
then he spent some time manipulating you to stay
you didn't give up on him
you gave in to God's voice
and you realized that you were worthy of the choice
the one that he was a fool for not making
you didn't give up
you were just over not being chosen

what kills me most.

I think what kills my heart the most

is that you're the one who showed me

what Jesus was all about

you were the one who brought me to know who He is

you showed me what it looked like

to live my life for His name

I think that's what kills my heart the most

<u>k e e p   a w a y .</u>

I'm feeling okay today
I guess that's what I need
to finally feel good with being okay
it's been so long since I've felt this way
I don't even know how I'm supposed to actually feel
is this even real?

God is here with me
with Him, I know I'll find all the answers I need
that's what keeps me away from going back to you
and your sick tortured ways

s h i n e   s t e a l e r .

I don't get how you can go so long without me

maybe you just needed room to breathe

I thought by now you'd realize what you missed

I can't even remember what it's like to feel your kiss

I think of your face,

but I can't even remember that place

I forgot the details already

I can barely even remember your eyes

they use to shine like gold

but somewhere along the line

the drug took that shine

just like everything else

that plant killed our dreams

I just wish you could see

but I get it, you're so high

it's hard to see anything clear

when you're so far from here

it's not fair, you get to escape

it's not okay

I know you're just hiding behind the hurt

I know you think you've smoked too much

but you're never too far gone

where Jesus won't take you back

He wants you more than I ever did

I pray one day that's something you'll see

5 : 3 0 a m   t h o u g h t .

what if God wants to take me higher,

no substance required,

just surrender?

c l o s e t   c r i e s .

it's a new year now, still the same broken me

I've come to terms with the fact

that you don't want me

I still haven't heard from you

I can't help but think it's Gods protection

you're too lost in your sin

I keep hoping you call

I still can't eat

my closet floor turns into the place I go to cry

why do I feel like I want an actual goodbye?

<u>a l w a y s .</u>

He sees you in your mess

He's been there the entire time

He's there

He's not going anywhere

a Savior's love.

these bitter winter days are dwindling away

I know God wants in on my heart these days

I know He sees me falling apart

I claimed to be a follower of His name,

but all I can feel is so much shame

I know He's the only One

who can put me together again

I can't help but think

hasn't He seen all my sin?

doesn't He know how long it's been

since I've truly lived my life for His name?

I've been so caught up

could His love still be the same?

y o u ' r e   n o t   s o r r y .

I get a message from you, of course I do

it comes out of the blue, I knew it was coming

but it wasn't in the way it wanted to

you try blaming me for the mess you made

you say you're not always going to

be doing things this way

you claim you won't always have to have a buzz

you're not the same and I can hear it in your voice

yet somehow I still want to be your choice

you say one day you'll change, but we both know

that I've heard all of this before

you still don't apologize

you have yet to own up to what you've done

because let's face it

we both know you're still not done having fun

8 : 0 0 a m   o n   a   M o n d a y .

the days are colder than ever

it's Monday morning and I can't get out of bed

my feet won't move from under the covers

my brain tells them to move

but my heart says no

I thought this part was done

why can't I get you out of my head

and leave this bed?

I know I'm still healing

but I figured I was done

with the air escaping my lungs

and the strength leaving my limbs

I thought the ache in my heart

had healed enough for me to breathe

I start crying

and the tears fall as all of my fears seep into my sheets

I'm so tired

I'm past exhausted

I haven't heard from you

I know God keeps protecting me

but I just want to hear how you've been

I worry about you

why do I care

when you stopped so long ago?

I want you to change

why isn't God moving here

why?

I cry

and then I realize, things will never be the same

I guess I'll never be worth it to you

s w a l l o w e d   w h o l e .

I fill the bathtub again tonight

I light a candle

it's just another night here without you

the water is hotter than it should be

but if I'm honest, I do that part on purpose

I step in and it's way too hot, why did I do that?

it burns, but I submerge myself anyway because even

if it's fleeting, it's numbing to this ache in my heart

eventually it cools down

and the numbing sensation fades

the steam gets heavy, it's almost too thick

it rises as the candle burns its wick

I can barely see my hands in front of me

the silence pierces the air

this is my place to escape

there's no one here

I feel too bare

too broken

I feel empty

I feel sick

I miss you

wait no, I miss who you were

I don't even know who you are anymore

I close my eyes and think about how it felt with your

arms around me and it makes my heart sore

you don't care

you never really did

I wrap my arms around my waist

it's so much smaller these days

it's so thin, so bare

it's as if I'm not even there

only because I haven't eaten a real meal in weeks

I can't describe this feeling in my brain

it makes me feel like I'm going insane

I feel like I'm being swallowed whole

I have no strength in me anymore

I just want to stay here

the only thing I know how to do is cry

sometimes I honestly feel like I just want to die

I often think how much better heaven would be

how can I possibly keep doing this?

I close my eyes and go under the water to escape

I hold my breath

just long enough to distract myself from the pain

that's going on inside my brain

I need to breathe

I know I need to come up for air

why would I though?

when the situation that I'm facing

up there is so far from fair?

I come up to get a breath

then the tears start falling and fast

I pray this feeling doesn't last

I can't help but scream

this is so much worse than

all of the movies ever made it seem

i t w o n ' t a l w a y s .

I hope you know that in your moments

where the darkness feels like it's caving

and it just might swallow you whole

you've got Someone

the One to pull you out of it

no matter how hard satan pushes you

into the hot water

God is right there pulling you out

let the tears fall

it's okay

just breathe

the burning will pass

that ache in your soul will stop one day

I know it feels as if it has settled

into every corner of your body

your heart feels heavy

your bones feel weak

your stomach feel empty

your brain feels achy

but it won't always be like this

it really, really won't

the water will cool down soon

just breathe

m o u r n i n g   y o u .

it's not going back to the way it was

who you were and who you are

they are two different people

I can see it

even though my tears keep blurring my vision

letting us fall apart was your decision

I can't keep doing this and now I know

I have to mourn the death of the guy I once loved

this is the hardest place

that my heart will have to go

grieving the death of someone

who is still alive, but no longer the guy I know

phone stares.

silence fills the air between us still

you never called, you probably never will

it hurts my heart more than you know

I never thought you'd be okay with letting me go

I lay in bed

running through all of it in my mind

I stare at my phone

wanting it to ring

but the screen stays dark

just like where you left us

roots need water too.

I don't know why I think about this,
but sometimes I do
this way of thinking that you thought was okay
you'd say that you already put in your time with me
you claimed to have planted our roots
but you didn't have time to give them any more life
you wanted to go deeper with your own dreams
the ones that stopped including me
but didn't you know
that our roots needed water to go deeper too?

v a n   n e s s   a v e n u e .

remember those days,

in that cute little studio by the bay?

we paid way too much for rent and ate those burgers

with the eggs that were heaven sent

it was short, but it was sweet

it's the only memories I've chosen to keep

I guess because it's the last time I remember

ever feeling truly loved by you

I don't know what else to do

so I lock them up inside a safe place

that I've made in my heart

it's a tiny little corner where I allow my mind visit

when I don't want to remember

that you tore the rest of it apart

memory flashes.

of course you have a few good memories left
and you get to decide, will they control you?
don't let the flash of a good memory make you forget
the reality of who he really is

s o a k e d   i n   s m o k e .

what made you stop loving me?

I think about it and it makes my heart ache

maybe it was when you began to feel like the money

was making you happier than I did

I guess that plant just offered you a better deal

something that could make you numb to feel

it was the easy way to make good money

more than you'd know what to do with

so I guess that's when it happened

when your bloodstream got soaked in the smoke

and you started chasing a dream

that reflected pure greed

that's when you stopped loving me

g o n e .

it helps recognizing that you're really gone

it's easier this way

what do you when someone dies?

you move on

you go forward

you have no other choice right?

that's what I have to do

and I know that now

I have to go on as if you're dead

because you are

the man I once loved

the man who loved Jesus

the man who showed me so long ago

what love really was

he's gone and passed

I take a deep breath and get on with my life

I can't stay here anymore

I know this pain won't last

I need room to breathe

I'm going home to my Creator

when he gets high, you feel low.

he doesn't see that the choices

he's making are destroying you

you tell him that he's hurt you

and yet you're the one who says you're sorry

why do you keep giving him the benefit of the doubt?

you have too good of a heart

you're always the one apologizing

you're always trying to see the best in him

you don't want to believe the worst

you see the best because it's how you want to be seen

for everything you're capable of being

yet he doesn't want to be seen like that

because that means he has to

give up control to his Creator

and he feels like he needs control

he breathes for control

because at the end of the day

in the dark of the night

his soul feels out of control

so he gets high to try and get it back

he's got you living a life of substance soaked highs

and alternating abusive lows

don't settle for that kind ride in life

get off that rollercoaster

a h e a r t a t r e s t .

weeks have come and went

doing life with Jesus these days

is all that keeps me together

it's almost Spring

the cold's almost over

I hate the cold

I want the sun

I know it's just a season

I can see things clearer

you use to live for Jesus, but that guy is long gone

I still think about the fact that I never got a goodbye

and in the back of my mind

it hurts in a way that's a different kind

it hurts, but it's okay because I know it's best

God won't keep anything from me unless

it won't put my heart at rest

l o v e   l e s s o n s .

I know now that you can only love me

as well as you love yourself

and when you don't truly love Jesus

you don't really know yourself

and when you don't know yourself

you won't know how to love me

r e s t a r t .

I can finally breathe a little better

the nights are still hard

the pain still stings

but not as much as it use to

running towards God has been my saving grace

I don't know where I'd be without His love

He's never going to leave me

He's here and I know I'm not alone

He's just building me into

the woman I was meant to be

I know He's using the broken pieces of my heart

just to give me a sweet restart

I feel as if I'm moving into the middle

far from where I use to be

but not yet where He has prepared for me

I don't know what's next

I don't know what my purpose even is

but I do know that I lost myself in

trying to love you in the middle of your sin

0 2 . 0 6 .

I knew the day was coming

but I didn't think much of it

I've been getting back to me

it wasn't a date that I let my heart focus on to see

it would have been six years today and

suddenly my stomach is sick

my body is aching in so much pain

I think it's just a stomach ache

I wait to see if it will pass

but for some reason the pain comes again and fast

it sits right under my ribs

the pain twists and turns inside me

as if I were having a kid

it hurts more than I can take

I've never felt this kind of ache

I lay on the floor, crying in fear

not knowing what in the world is going on here

I thought it was something I ate

but the truth is I haven't eaten much to date

the pain gets worse as my phone rings by my side

it's a text from you and I think to myself

of course today you don't hide

I haven't heard from you in weeks

and today you choose to reach out

I read the message on the screen

I want to throw up with the words I've seen

you say you're thinking of me today

that you're sending good vibes my way

what does that even mean?

I want to scream

I want to shout

but I'm in so much pain

my insides are cringing as I cling to the carpet

trying to stay sane

I don't know what's going on here

I know God's with me and I have nothing to fear

I call for help, the doctors run tests for hours

they come back later with nothing to say

they don't know where the pain is coming from

it's a mystery in their heads

but I know it's because you're back from the dead

my body was just responding to this day

and not in the way I ever thought

did you really think that was okay

to send a message like that

like you've done nothing wrong?

you've been fine without me for this long

yet just because I'm sick you offer to come see me

you ask me what I need

I want to scream

all I ever needed was for you to choose me

the rest of the night is a blur

the doctor gives some kind of magic potion

she says it should put me to sleep

like the sound of the ocean

but it makes me want to throw up

I get home and hallucinate as I fall asleep

and just like you

the pain came and went

as if it were never mine to keep

a damaged heart.

I hate to think it, but I sometimes do

who could ever love a damaged heart like mine?

what if they really knew?

I have this broken past

I thought I had something that would last

the rhythm.

Winter is fading away.

I thank God it's a season that doesn't stay

my heart is finding its rhythm again

God only knows how long it's been

I fear loving some new

yet I wear my heart on my sleeve

because it's all I know how to do

spring.

little fighter.

I know sometimes it's hard to see

the plans that God has for me

but I know I just need to let it be

He has it this way for a reason

I'm meant to bloom into something beautiful

through this season

I feel like my heart is lighter

I've somehow become God's little fighter

I feel free

my chains have come undone

I'm somewhere in between

I don't know where I'm going

I can't see my purpose

I wish God would make it clear

but in my heart, I feel like I'm getting near

I can see now that God's glory

is worth the pain in my story

it was worth the nights of nearly going insane

I used to feel so trapped in my thoughts
I've had so many words to say
but they've been stuck in my head because you
always made me feel like they were never okay
I know now that I have to get them out
when I spill my words, I can breathe
it's been so long since I've actually
been able to breathe
I need to breathe
my heart needs to write this feeling

g o o d   s l e e p .

the more I write
the better I sleep at night

h u n g r y   a g a i n .

I'm more me than I've ever been

I can sleep through the night

my stomach has even begun to find its appetite

I don't know what's ahead

I know I want to see this world

I want to get lost in the places that I've always

dreamed about in my head

life is just better when God has the pen

I can see that now and He's taking me

somewhere that I've never been

I don't know how we're getting there

but maybe that's the point

I need to let my Creator consume my heart

because whether I like it or not

I know He's set me apart

c l o s u r e   i s n ' t   r e a l .

I heard from you again today

you have nothing new to say

you want closure now

yet you still haven't said you're sorry

you don't think you've done anything wrong

you're just replaying your same old song

you don't regret losing me

I know you're just too high to see

all of the damage you've done to me

you can't understand that you've lost me for good

I don't think you'll ever realize the pain

that you put me through

you still send these texts out of the blue

but yet nothing new is being said

what we had is dead

you're the one who let it die so easily

right in front of your eyes

you're going over the past

like you want me to apologize for not making it last

I tell you I'm moving on

if you need the closure to get it now

I'm real because that's just how my heart feels

I wish you the best

I give you a chance to say the rest

and you do what you do best

you disappear without a word

leaving me and my heart to guess

weak knees.

it happened one day so suddenly

I crossed paths with someone new

he literally came out of the blue

I felt a tap on my shoulder

and right then my heart felt like it was game over

he got my hearts attention from the start

I didn't know how hard it'd be

a few weeks spent

and he became all my heart could see

we spent hours that day

we never ran out of something to say

we talked for hours

he told me his story

I opened up my heart

his presence made me feel at ease

every time I'd look at him, I'd get weak in my knees

i d e a s   v s .   r e a l i t y .

you brought out a side of me

that I forgot was even there

it felt like maybe you actually cared

but you moved away

yet you kept me hanging on by a string

just long enough so I'd stay

you took some time

you looked at me with a certainty in your eyes

it was clearly nothing but lies

as if you were there for real

but I should have known better

little boys don't really know how they feel

it's almost as if you've done this before

leaving hearts like mine feeling confused and sore

I should have known

when you could never find the words to say

that you didn't want me

you wanted the idea of who we could be

all while I sat there with my heart on my sleeve

current location.

somewhere between

where I've been

and where I'm going

g e t t i n g   t o   k n o w   Y o u .

they say travel is good for the soul

so I'm leaving for three weeks

I've got a heavy heart

it's one that longs to be loved

loved by the One who made it

I've never known what that really feels like

I feel like it's time that I do

I really just want to get to know every part of You

h o n g   k o n g   f e e l i n g s .

I'm so far from where I've been

I walk around these streets

and for the first time in weeks

I'm feeling so free

I don't remember the last time it ever felt this good

to be alone and fully be able to see

there's so much more to life

so much more that matters

I feel my heart's getting lighter

the burden was never mine to carry

u p p e r h o u s e   v i e w s

something sacred is happening here
you're dancing through life with Me
and you look as beautiful as ever
you finally let Me sweep you off your feet
and now there's a shift within your heart
can't you feel it?
it's finding its true rhythm

-God to me, maybe to you too

l a t e   n i g h t   t h o u g h t .

timing actually is everything

s h a n g h a i   8 : 0 0 p m .

the city lights up

it's the prettiest thing I've seen yet

I'm alone here with You and

I know that You're love is my best bet

it's the sweetest thing I've felt yet

these lights are shining so bright

and I begin to feel You tell me

that this is what my heart is suppose to look like

blue skies.

just like the skies after a storm
it's clearing up

sea days.

at sea,
between China and Japan
with an aching heart
I'm caught in the tide
between who I was and who I am

so simple.

I'm in bed by 8

alone again, as I crawl under the sheets

I open Your word

I close my eyes

and I know by now

You're not one to hide

You're here

You're so near

I can feel it in my bones

the lights are low

but the room begins to sparkle

peace drowns my soul

I feel that You're here

I start to cry

because for the first time in so long

I feel loved

I feel whole

I feel new

You're presence is more than enough

t a i l o r   m a d e .

My light is shining out of you
because of this new heart I've put inside of you
and it's tailor made for the man
who will see the gold in you just like I do

- God to me, maybe to you too

a l l   i   w a n t   t o   d o .

shower people with His love like He's showered me

that's faith.

the not knowing what's around the corner

but going with Him anyway

believing that the highest blessing

He has for you is coming up

that's faith

y o u   a r e   w o r t h y .

you are worthy of a life
that lights you up from the inside out
you deserve to be really happy
you deserve dinners filled with laughter
you deserve nights rooted in love
you deserve really good conversation
you deserve a Godly man
you deserve peace and excitement
you are worthy of a life that radiates passion
despite what's happened to you
you are worthy of it all and so much more

c o f f e e   l o v e r s

the love you bring to the table is more than enough
so don't be afraid to have your coffee alone

s t o p   w o r r y i n g .

you are going to be
someone's best thing
someone's only thing
someone's sure thing
someone's pretty little thing
someone's forever thing
don't you worry your pretty little mind

just different.

I'm home now

and I feel so completely different

but I feel like me

but it feels like I'm different

because I haven't felt this way in so long

I really am enough

I don't know why they don't always stay

but I'm beginning to see that maybe it's okay

because I believe now that

God's the one who has it that way

p r o m i s e .

your prayers didn't get swallowed up by the darkness
they have simply been sown into the night

n o w   l o o k .

want to really appreciate it
want to figure out what it really means to you
be without for a little while
as long as it takes
don't rush. don't hurry. just be
now look, what to do you see?

I s r a e l i t e   f e e l s .

the trees are starting to bloom

it's almost June

I feel God here,

He's steering my heart towards His plans for me

it's not easy, doing things this way

I can see now why back in the day

the Israelites didn't want to stay

it'd be easier to go back

but I know for a fact there's nothing there for me

there was never closure

there was never a goodbye

I wonder if he thinks about me from time to time

it's a dead thing, it has no more life,

and yet it still sears pain into my heart every night

summer.

season change up.

Spring is over

the trees are in full bloom

it's nearly June

I didn't think it'd get here this soon

it's been half a year since

I left him in so much fear

I didn't think I'd get here

but it's sweeter than I dreamed it'd be

it's everything I'll ever need

Summer is here

and my heart is the Lords to keep

He's swept me off my feet

He's had every guy beat

I'm so good here

I have nothing to fear

Summer's finally here

Christmas in June.

he wanted you like that toy he desired all year long

and once he gets to hold you

he'll play you

making you feel like his new favorite song

like you're special

just until the newness is gone

then he will throw you to the side

leaving you behind

wanting something new

making you think that

there's something wrong with you

but there's not

you were not created to be toyed with

you were created to be treasured

u n w a n t e d   f e e l i n g s .

I thought you were different

I had hope that you'd be good to my heart

after all, you knew how bruised it was from the start

but I guess I was too dumb too think

that everyone has a good heart like me

I didn't ask to catch feelings

I wish you would have stayed away

when you left that day

I always had so much more to say

I should have known

I should have guessed

that a boy like you

couldn't handle me at my best

s w e e t   t o o t h .

he was bored

he was lonely

he was selfish

walk away

don't text him

don't entertain his childish brain

be careful from now on okay?

I know you believe to see the best

in every guy you meet

it's only because you're far too sweet

please don't let him in the door

when his craving comes back

once he gets bored

ew, déjà vu.

I see you one last time

you say hello, but you treat me like a total stranger

as if somehow I brought some kind of danger

you really think it's okay to treat a woman this way?

I want to talk, yet there's something in your heart

that's causing a block

I can't believe after everything

that you'd treat me this way

you can't man up and find a single word to say?

I fade into the crowd that night

I can barely think

it's like you don't want to be found

and for a second your eyes meet mine

as if we're both searching for the answers

we want to find

I have to get out

I feel like I can't breathe

I tell you I'm leaving

you say goodbye with a simple nod

as I feel the pieces of my heart shatter inside

I should have known

looks can be deceiving

I walk away trying to hold my head high

all while the tears well up behind my eyes

my heart hurts with each step I take

I guess that's what I get for opening it up to a fake

I find myself in my car again

I've been here before and it feels too sore

I know what's about to happen

the tears are coming in hot

I start my car in a hurry to get out of the parking lot

I can't let you see me cry

you won't care

you never did

let's be honest

you are too much of a little kid

a rare heart.

I thought I meant more

I thought he loved like you Lord

I know now he's just too immature to see

how rare my heart is and always will be

f i l l   i n   t h e   b l a n k .

what hurts the most is that you left without a word

and now you're making me play fill in blank

as the silence fills the air

it makes me realize that you never truly cared

I don't understand where I went wrong

for a minute, I feel like I wasn't worth the choice

but I know that's only the enemy's voice

God has a different plan for me

one that I still can't see

I know there's more ahead

I just wish at least one word could have been said

it just feels so lost and dead

same story, different day.

don't let his inability to see how amazing you are

think you need to change

there's nothing wrong with you

the problem isn't you

the problem is him

he doesn't know what he wants

he doesn't know who he really is

he's too caught up with what other people think

he's concerned with his image

it's the same story

just a different day

don't go thinking you need to change

you're worth it

d r e a m g i r l .

because of you

I know now when to say no

you couldn't see the value I bring

I guess you were just playing for a different team

but I'm good, I know I'm loved by the King

there's no use in dwelling over the past

if you valued me

you wouldn't have let me get away so fast

you're just a boy who dreams of having a girl like me

but I'm gone now, so you can stop checking up on me

you had me right there

yet all you could do was stare

exit this way.

him giving you silence doesn't mean you get louder,
it means you walk away that much quieter.

how life turned out.

it's everything I never imagined,
and yet it's so much sweeter.

p r e p a r a t i o n .

I know God's got a plan for me

I've been alone long enough

to know that it's all preparation

I don't know what for

I've learned so much

I know better now

I'm better because of the breaking

I don't regret being so open

I don't regret being honest

I don't regret being real

hey at least I can feel

I know what it's like to be broken

I know what it's like to be lead on

I know what it's like to be loved one minute

and forgotten about the next

I don't always get why they leave

why I'm not worth keeping

I guess it's for a reason

maybe I'll understand why next season

 | o | .

he thought you'd come back.

c o m e   t h r o u g h .

I can feel it in my bones
the way God's working now
He's moving in my soul
and seeping into the corners of my heart
where I thought it was all too far gone and torn apart
He's made me like new
He's taken away the fear
has He always been this near?

maybe He never left
I know now that He's not like the rest
His promises are true
and unlike you
He actually comes through

s o m e t h i n g   b e t t e r .

sometimes being torn apart is good

I know it hurts more than anything in the moment

but He's going to build you

into something better

something good

something beautiful

you just have to let Him

it will be painful

it will hurt

it will be uncomfortable

it will be harder than anything you've ever had to do

but it's worth it, to find out what God already knew

a l l   i   s e e .

I finally feel free

I'm more of the woman

that my Savior has called me to be

I have no need to flee

God's love is all around me

it's all I see

I've waited patiently to get to this place

and now I'm wrapped up in His embrace

t h e p l a c e s y o u ' l l g o

go places where you feel free

where you can breathe

where you can be with Me

where you hear Me best

where you can truly rest

- God to me, maybe to you too

s o c u t e .

don't fall for his words

talk is cute

action is what actually matters

don't be a fool

watch what he does

not what he says he'll do

solo.

maybe God's love really is enough

be okay with being alone

you're so much stronger than you think.

a c t i o n   t y p e .

even after everything
I somehow still believe in true love
I'm not afraid to be alone
I know one day I will reap what I've sown
until then I'm by myself
and I prefer it that way
I know better than to just believe
the words that they say
actions are what matter in the end
and honestly I probably only want to be your friend
yet I still wear my heart on my sleeve
praying the next one who comes
into my life doesn't leave

s o w n   p r a y e r s .

I know one day

the one You have for me will stay

I'm not worried that I'll end up alone

I believe everything You say

I'm just not sure how long it'll take

and how will I know who is a fake?

I guess that's what scares me the most

not being able to know if he's the one that

You've sent as the answer to the prayers I've sown

b e t t e r   a l o n e .

I do feel like I can breathe

it seems easier on my own

I hated that thing where I always waited by my phone

I used to wait for it to ring

like he was some sort of king

I'm past that now

it's just me and You

yet sometimes my heart turns to a shade of blue

I know I like to be alone

I'm honestly too scared to let my heart be shown

smoke paths.

I'm living God's way now

I know He's got something big up His sleeve

I just don't want another one to leave

I don't think my heart could take that pain

I just might go insane

I hate it because sometimes I think about him

how he's doing

living in that sin

and when the smell of smoke comes across my path

I inhale and think back

is that strange?

I know a scent or a song always brings

you back to a certain place

sadly the smell of the green

now reminds me of all the evil I've seen

whether it's a stranger passing by or

when I'm driving down the street

that smell is one that gives my heart an ache

and for a second it skips a beat

I hate that I remember him that way

but it's the only memory I have left from that day

I know I have the ones from that studio by the bay

but like every sunset, they just keep fading away

e x h a l i n g   m e m o r i e s .

don't let a memory of him slip into your heart

and destroy your peace

he left you alone to deal with this pain

don't go thinking of him and wonder if he's changed

if he did

he'd be there

but he's not

you deserve someone who will be there for you

not someone who says he wants to

but doesn't come through

keep breathing

exhale the memories

t i m e   t i c k s .

I can't help but think,

does your heart ever stop feeling the pain?

from the heartbreak, it has to go away

I used to think that time heals all wounds

now I know that's just not true

if time was all it took

he'd be someone by now that my heart never knew

but time doesn't heal

time just reveals

then we get to decide

just how much we feel

how much we hide

how much we conceal

how much we suffer

how much we cry

how much we can take till we really let go

and say goodbye

a l e a k y   h e a r t .

it's okay you still think about him

that's the good in your heart that's leaking out

don't think you're weak because he crosses your mind

he's weak for not being able to love you

c o n f u s i n g   c o n f u s i o n .

if he's not making an effort

he doesn't really care

he doesn't care about your feelings

he's confused and it's confusing you

don't let his inability to know himself

keep you from loving someone else

there's someone out there who

is looking for a sweet love like yours

your heart is too good

and he's confused

he's not the man your heart deserves

h e a r t   d r e a m s .

maybe in the future we could be right

you could turn into the man

who eventually puts up the fight

and maybe you'd realize by then

that I was all your heart ever really dreamed about

and the success didn't really matter

if it meant leaving us and my heart to shatter

t h e   r e a l   o n e .

and that's the thing about a woman like me

I'll bring out every weak man's insecurities

because I know Whose I am

I know what I want

I won't settle

I'll wait – as long as it takes

I'm not afraid to be alone

I'll never put myself in that position again

I've come too far from where I've been

l a y e r s   o f   l o v e .

wait for the one who knows

how to love your layers

[u n] c o n d i t i o n a l l o v e .

Your love is better than what this world gives

no one will ever be able to love me like You do

You're unfailing

You're unchanging

Your love is unconditional

it's so sweet

to be swept off my feet

I stayed in a love that turned

into a place with conditions

now I can see that wasn't Your mission

n o t   a b o u t   m e .

it's not about me

it's not about how big I can be

it's not about how much money I make

it's not about the clothes I wear

it's not about the places I see

it's not about me in the slightest bit

it's all about His name

all the glory and all the fame

Jesus brought me so far

I won't ever forget those days in my car

the times when the tears stung my eyes

all because I let my heart believe your lies

d e s e r v i n g   o f   l o v e .

you're so use to being mistreated

that being treated well actually scares you

you feel like a burden

but you're not

you think because he pays for you

that you'll owe him something later

but you don't

you worry that you won't be enough

but you are

you wonder how long it'll take till he gives up on you

but he won't

you have to get use to the fact

that you deserve to be loved

w o r t h y   f o r   k e e p s .

it's hard doing things on my own

I wonder if he ever thinks about picking up the phone

I think about it from time to time

I almost do

but then God quickly reminds me of the facts

and I know I can't go back

so I smile and breathe in deep

remembering all of it will be worth doing life

with the one who sees that I'm worthy enough to keep

r e a l   d e s i r e .

I'm doing this by myself

I've forgotten the feeling of falling in love

I long just to be held

my body and soul craves a love like fire

I want to be fully known

and completely loved

that's my heart's real desire

I just want someone who stays

who doesn't leave when it

gets messy in the grey

in between days.

just because you've been alone for awhile

don't play with other people's hearts

you know what it's like to be so hurt

don't flirt with a fling when it's not a God thing

c l e a r   c h o i c e s .

why do I miss you today?

why do I do this to myself?

letting my heart wander past the edge

I know it's not always going to be this way

I understand it will pass

I just wish sometimes you'd reach out

for a minute, I wish we could talk

say the things we never got to say

it hurts, knowing it's all stuck in the in between

doesn't it hurt your heart?

then I remember why this silence fills the air

and it's because you left that thread without a reply

you made the choice to leave with no goodbye

you made it seem so easy

you made it so clear

losing me wasn't something you feared

h i g h l i g h t   r e e l .

he's an extrovert

you're an introvert

he's insecure in his emotions

you're secure in how you feel

so that's why he runs and hides

behind his highlight reel

when the feelings get real

he doesn't know how to handle

a real woman like you

because he's still yet to face

the real struggle going on behind the scenes

the outtakes that no one gets to see

so he goes from girl to girl

making them all weak in the knees

just trying to fill a void in his heart

it's one that's been there for awhile

that's why he acts like such a child

he's facing more than anyone knows

he's doing it on his own

he misses his family back home

but yet he rarely picks up the phone

you wonder why he avoids it all

why he can't even call

he sold you on some false hope

it's his way of numbing the pain to cope

and you bought into it, thinking it was true

but he well knew that soon enough

he'd be done with you too

it's not your fault he can't face the battle inside

don't be like him, don't run and hide

feel what you feel and then walk away

you'll learn by doing so

it's better when you let God have the final say

b i b l e   f o o d .

he left you in silence

so easily, he walked away

don't you remember the pain that day?

you don't need a conversation with him

you need to keep talking to your Creator

God has the comfort you need

yes, the ache in your heart will be sore

but don't go back to him thinking it will help things

he left you to deal with it on your own

don't be the girl who goes to him

when the starvation kicks in

put your phone away and

open your Bible instead

His words are the ones that you need to truly be fed

make sure.

with love as deep as the ocean,
you better make sure he can swim.

don't depend on.

an apology from him,
applause from them.

b a y   d a y s .

when I think back to how we use to be

my mind goes straight to those the days

before we moved back from the bay

it's like they've been etched

into my heart with permanent ink

and it's driving me crazy not knowing what you think

ink dreams.

I write these words and it feels like I'm bleeding

with every part of being

my heart is splattered on this page

for far too long you made me keep them

locked up in a cage

and now that I'm free

I don't know if I'll ever run out of words to say

I write so easily these days

it has always been my dream

writing about the things unseen

my heart feels free, my chains are broken

all because my Savior never gave up on me

I've come so far from where I've been

I never want to stop chasing these dreams with Him

s m i l i n g   f o r   r e a l .

you only cared about your dreams

you filled them with the money

it's clear that your soul got stuck in the honey

no wonder it was so hard for me

to get through to your heart

I should have known

you never cared that you tore mine apart

I'm here now and

I'm finally smiling for real

I can easily breathe, I can clearly see

I'm the woman you thought I never could be

n e v e r l e a v i n g .

God's given me so much in this life

His power is real

His presence is near

His promises are true

He loves me so much more than I ever knew

He gets my heart

He knows the pain

He cares

He's not going anywhere

f l o o d   g a t e s .

I keep feeling this need to get it all out
I don't want to regret not putting it down
when the words come into my head
they come like a flood
rushing out of my fingertips and onto the screen
I'll forever be happy writing about the things unseen

h e a r t b r e a k
g i v e s   y o u   w i n g s .

I keep seeing butterflies everywhere I go
it's reminding me that I've found my wings
as I keep turning into the woman that
God's been building me to be
it took all four seasons
and my soul feels so light
I know I just had to surrender it all
and put down the fight

n e e d   v s .   w a n t .

the burden was never yours to carry

just because he didn't choose you

it doesn't mean you're not worthy

you scare him because you're whole all by yourself

you didn't need him

you wanted him

there was a difference

he simply couldn't handle you at your best

so now he will end up with something less

someone mediocre at best

l o v e .

my love is deep

my love is rare

my love is for keeps

my love is real

my love is the kind that really makes your heart feel

feel the things that you don't always want to face

it's a love that you won't ever have to chase

it's the kind of love that wakes up with you on a

Monday and loves you all the way to next Sunday

f o r g i v e n e s s   f e e l s .

how do you forgive someone

who never said they were sorry?

one season ago

I asked God this question every day

I'd play it over in my mind

how do you forgive someone

who hurt you so many times?

it didn't seem fair

he so easily left without a care

months pass and he still lets the silence fill the air

it was childish

it was selfish

it was cruel

he made me feel like such a fool

I've learned so much since then

I can see now that the forgiveness

was never about him

it was about my own heart

even though he was the one

who let me go and tore it apart

God only wanted me to go

so that He could heal me

and show me everything that He already knows

s t i c k y   s i t u a t i o n s.

when people ask what happened to you and me
I tell them that it was simple really
he fell in love with the money
while I refused to let my heart get stuck like his did
in that dream killing honey

a fire realization.

staying in love is a choice

you chose him too many times

when he forgot to choose you

you used to be in love

you'd give up the world for him

you did give up the world

but now you can breathe because you realize

that you do want the best for him

but you're done with the games

now you're free from that desire

because God has lit your heart up

with a different kind of fire

m e .

it feels good to smile and feel like it's true

for so long I faked it and no one ever knew

they didn't know the pain

they didn't know the games you played

I thank God He rescued me

this freedom is sweeter than anything

even when I'm alone

I'm awake

I'm alive

I'm me

I'm known

to my future husband.

I miss you

I think about you everyday

I wonder where you are

I think about your heart

tell me, how many times has it been torn apart?

is it like mine?

I pray for you every night

you're the last one I think about

even when my heart's putting up a fight

I can't wait to hear your laugh

I'm dying to see your smile

I think about your hugs

doesn't it feel like it's been a while?

I think about how your kiss will feel

I get this feeling that it won't even seem real

I don't know where you are

I don't know how far we have to go

but thinking about you now makes me cry

because to me, I'm so excited that you're my guy

I don't want anyone else

I know I seem crazy to wait

I keep saying no to all the other dates

I don't know what you look like

I don't know where you are on earth today

all I know is that one day

when we're together

it's finally going to feel more than okay

same heart.

I find peace in the Word

it's the only book I open and feel my soul breathe

I know life is fleeting

I know I'm doing things right

but at night, I still feel the fight

the grasp I want to have on my life

the not knowing what's next can get exhausting

I know I have to let God be God

I only want what He has for me

but sometimes I can't help but question

doesn't He see?

o n   t h e   f r e n c h s i d e .

I'm home now

feeling free to do everything

and more that He created me for

my words matter

I've never been too much

although I can't help but wonder

where does a heart like mine fit it in the bunch?

maybe that's what He wants

for me not to quite fit in with the rest of them

truth is I'm not the one with the pen

I don't know where we're going

I only know where I've been

c r a v i n g s .

I'm crying and I don't know why

I'm free and I'm okay

but I feel so lonely today

I wonder if it ever stops

thinking about you as it turns my stomach into knots

I crave a love that's real

I don't even know how it would feel

I know what it's like to be loved by

the One from above

but from a man down here?

that's something I can't help but fear

my heart hurts

I can't imagine it

it scares me because all I know from an earthly love

is the kind that destroyed me from the inside out

I only have the words for what I know

I hate that I can't write what true love is really like

maybe one day I will

when His plans are revealed

it will all make sense

why He needed me here

so content

sweet kisses.

you're afraid of what it might feel like

to actually be loved

by a man, not a boy

you don't even know what that would

be like and it scares you

it'll be a new thing for your heart

peace will settle there

laughter will fill the air

there will be so many sweet kisses he will take

your soul will be even more alive and awake

confusion will not be relevant

playing mind games will not be apart of the deal

you will be shocked at how true love is going to feel

j u s t   b e   r e a l .

for the briefest moment

I find myself thinking of you

the thought of what we could have been

makes my heart ache

why couldn't you have said goodbye

why didn't you want to try?

I guess I can't keep asking myself

these things everyday

I deserve so much more

I'm letting go of this notion that you care

because I know if you did, you wouldn't leave

this silence hanging in the air

I'm tired of the games they all play

the silent one kills me the most

I hate when people can't just say how they feel

I'm always so honest

is it too much to just be real?

I can't understand why you bottle all of it up inside

and then choose to run away and hide

I guess I won't ever understand

because you were never a real man

t h e   p u s h   a n d   p u l l .

I feel like I'm torn between

this ache for the past

and the plan that my Savior has for me

b e t t e r   o f f .

you'll never get this moment back

this place right here

take it for everything it is

hold on to it tight because it's never

going to be this way again

you're so good on your own

you're whole by yourself

God's love brought you here

you have nothing to fear

it's going to be okay

the plans He has for you are better than you think

you're so much better off this way

e x h a u s t e d .

I love this new me

it's who I know God always has called me to be

it still hurts though

when I think about my past

the ache crawls into my mind

it makes a home in my head

wait, I thought those feelings were dead

he left, he doesn't care

I have to stop trying to figure out what he's thinking

I wasn't too much, I was too good

I wasn't too little, he just wasn't enough

I'm breathing in, I'm breathing out

I'm doing everything it takes not to shout

shout in anger, shout in pain

shout in exhaustion from this mental game

it doesn't hurt like it use to

it's not like I want him back

I cringe at the thought of living with him in his sin

h o p e f u l .

waiting for God to move

I don't know where I'm going

I know He's here

He's always so much closer than He appears

I feel like I've been lost at sea

despite it all

He's still here with me

I know we'll get where we're going when we do

I simply can't wait to see

everything that He already knew

a new song.

I want to write about the things that mean more

I want someone to read my writing and feel free

I want my words to pour into their soul

and make them feel known

I know it's what I'm meant to do

I never could have done this

had I stayed in that toxic place with you

you had me so twisted in your cycle of your sin

I know we all mess up in life

we don't always get it right

I'm far too guilty of doing things wrong

but now God's given me a new song

I can't look back now

I won't turn around

these words in my heart are just too loud

I don't want what's behind me anymore

I finally feel my feet moving away from the shore

n o   g o o d b y e .

I've come to terms with the fact

that maybe sometimes we don't get goodbye

sometimes, we just get our God's love

and that's more than enough

that's what I've learned through my mess

a goodbye doesn't change a thing

besides, he still thinks he's some sort of king

I can breathe so much easier, untangled from his sin

greater things.

God's got greater things for me in store

it's so clear to see and impossible to ignore

I can feel something sweeter is coming in the distance

that's why this all feels so great

being alone

knowing that what I'm doing has made me grow

I keep getting better everyday

I can't wait to be with the one who stays

the one who sees beneath all the layers

and loves me all the same

u s e   t o .

people ask me what I use to do

before I started writing

I tell them I use to say sorry

I use to make excuses for you

I use to be trapped

I use to be half loved

I use to never laugh

I use to keep my lips sealed

I use to conceal everything I would feel

I use to cry so much

I use to try to keep my body paper thin

I use to give in to living with you in your sin

I use to do your laundry

I use to make you food

before I started writing,

I guess I just use to be controlled by you

<u>a c t u a l l y   n o t   s o r r y .</u>

you always told me

I'd never be able to handle

a life with anyone successful

truth is you're the one who

couldn't have handled me if I was

you were insecure with yourself

you hid behind the money

you saw my potential

and you were afraid if I found it too

that I'd get sick of your games and leave you

so you did the only thing you knew how to do

you kept me boxed up like that doll

you kept me feeling small

but now I'm here

and for the first time ever

I say this without any fear,

sorry, but I'm actually not sorry

p u r e   j o y .

this love here with You

it's something I never imagined could be so sweet

I close my eyes and think about

how much You love me

it fills my soul with this peace

I can't quite explain it

the tears well up in my eyes

and it's all because You love me

more than any other guy

You love me here

You loved me then

You love me now, no matter where I've been

it feels good being so free

feeling the breeze and being so content

it's the best feeling in the world

getting to do this life with You Lord

it's all You ever wanted

it's what You had waiting for me

f o r e v e r   w a t e r i n g .

they say the grass isn't greener on the other side

it's green where you water it

but it takes two people for a relationship to work

and if only one person waters

while the other one stares

I wonder, how is that fair?

I'll never be the woman one who stops watering it

just because it gets hard

I've come too far

I'm over being half loved

I want to be awaken

I want to be shaken

I want to be alive for Your name

I don't want to play another boy's silly little game

t h e   t y p e   t o   k e e p   i t .

I think what keeps me going is the promise

because I know You're the type to keep it

You won't let it fade

even when it feels like You've forgotten

I just have to keep going

I think that's the hardest part

to wake up everyday without much changing

at least nothing I can see

I know you're working from above and that's key

it makes what doesn't make sense a little more clear

even though I'll admit, I sometimes slip into fear

I don't want to end up alone

I don't want to get it wrong

I want to go the right way

I want to let the right one in who will stay

I don't want to lose Your presence

I know I need you now more than ever

stay with me

please don't go

I don't want to get it wrong

I think that's what I fear so much

taking one step in the wrong direction

I never want what You don't have for me

I know now that You know so much better

You are the only One I see

I don't want to get hurt

my heart tightens inside at the thought

these words I speak are truer than true

I don't know what else to do

to get this out

sometimes I just want to shout

I have to get it all off my chest

the stress

the pain

the feeling like I'm the one losing

nearly going insane

I breathe in

I breathe out

I feel that You're here

I have nothing to lose

creative side.

your love story is only as creative

as you allow your Creator to create it

t h r o u g h   t h e   n i g h t .

I feel like a new woman these days

it's not easy though

people put me up as having it all together

they get one look at me from the outside

thinking that I have the perfect life

just because I'm always hoping on a flight

but they don't really know the war

that rages through the night

they don't know the pain that my heart feels

when the stars come out and all the layers start to peel

I'm just trying figure out where God wants me to go

most days, I don't even know

I don't know what my future holds

but I know Who has the pen

and He's the only one who keeps me

from going back to where I've been

o c e a n   l o v e .

you are an ocean,

it's not your fault that he didn't jump in

when God gave him the perfect opportunity to swim

r e q u i r e m e n t s .

you know better now

you know what's required

your love goes deeper than most

stop settling for a love

that doesn't want to leave the coast

r e s o n a t e .

all I want to do is lay in his arms

and by him, I mean the one God has for me

don't go thinking I wrote this part about you

it's clear by now that we've got very different views

did you ever really want us to work?

can I just be real?

you were the biggest jerk

now you can go thinking I wrote that part about you

because if you felt that it resonated

then it's probably true

truth is, I'm almost done with this book

then what do I do?

these pages are full of so many emotions

I feel like as soon as it's published

I'll want to dive into the ocean

escape from the scene of the reality that will be

not sure how you'll take this

for everyone to see

I don't mind because I know what I did was right

you're the one who will struggle now

sleeping through the night

I only spoke of what was true

I only wrote what we both knew

I pray this gets through to someone

and helps set them free

I hope they realize just how much happier

they deserve to be

h o m e   n o w .

looking back through all four seasons

each one was made up of something sweet

they all had their reasons

the reason for the pain

the reason for the mourning

the heart fights

the lonely nights

the solo flights

the restless days

it was just strengthening me

I see it all and it feels so good

just to be

I sit here without fear

I know You're here

You were here all along

giving my heart a sweet new song

n o b u z z n e e d e d .

for so long I put You on hold

I let my heart sit out with him in the cold

I ran away thinking I could do it on my own

when all along You were the One who had known

You knew the pain my heart was feeling

You saw my heart breaking and aching

You had the cure all along

I should have come home sooner

I'm sorry that I left

I thought I could get back

to something close to my best

but trying to do it on my own never works

I'll never go back to who I once was

I no longer need that buzz

Your love is the best

it will forever be where my soul can truly rest

I feel so good right here

You've always been this near

s x m .

I finally feel like I'm the woman you needed me to be

so that You can bring the things into my life that you

had always intended for me

it brings tears to my eyes

to know that You loved me this much

You always knew what my heart needed the most

I feel like from here I could do anything

I just want to go where You are

I want to feel Your presence with me

in everything I do

You make me feel brand new

like I'm worth the time

like I'm worth putting it all on the line

You're forever seeking me out

I don't want to leave this place

I've made Your heart my home

when my soul is tangled up with You,

it feels like a sweet day on the beach at noon.

f o o t s t e p s &
f i n g e r t i p s .

my fingertips hit the keyboard

and this unexplainable joy fills my soul

I feel like I'm on the brink of something so sweet

now it's all just a matter of where God places my feet

I'll go wherever He wants me to go

I'll sow whatever He needs me to sow

what i want.

everything God has for me and nothing He doesn't

daily aches.

I have an ache in my heart

for the real guy

who won't set me aside

i   a m .

my heart craves a love so deep

I wonder everyday

when will I be with the one who is going to stay?

I know You're directing our steps

You see the path better than I do

we're probably going the long way

knowing You

I'm honestly scared

to truly be loved again

only You know how long it's really been

I'm cautious

I'm patient

I'm tired

I'm lonely

I'm scared

I'm whole

I'm new

I'm exhausted

I'm free

true bliss.

Summer is in full swing now

I've never felt this good alone

doing things on my own

my roots have been planted in Your ways

I know ahead of me are my best days

Your love for me

is all my heart sees

it's all I'll ever need

b l a n k   s t a r e s .

I'm looking at things from a higher view

one that only God could show me

after making me brand new

I mean it when I say that I only want

the best for you these days

even after all the pain you put me through

my heart hopes you start living for Him again

only you and me know how long

it's really been since then

when I think about you, it still feels unfair

that you just left me at your front door with nothing

but a blank stare

I don't think it'll ever feel good anymore

the thought of you will always

leave my heart feeling sore

w i l d e r n e s s   w o n d e r .

they say the wilderness is a position of disfavor

however I can't help

but to disagree, can't you see?

in the wilderness with Him

you'll learn that His love is all you need

you'll get drenched with uncertainty

and tossed into the unknown

but wait for it, I promise

eventually you'll find your way back home

a b a c k r o a d l o v e .

the kind of love where you have to

take the back road to get there

it's going to be worth it in the end

so you really don't care

the type of love that doesn't just

come with a pretty view

but a with back story, all for God's glory

He has you going the long way

and somehow you just know

it's all going to be worth what you've sown

it will be worth the wait

it will be worth the struggle

it will be worth every lonely night

and when Jesus puts a detour in the road

you don't put up a fight

because you know now that it's leading you

to the one who will love you

from the morning, all the way into night

s i x   y e a r s   l a t e r .

craving something different,
I guess it's true what they say
taste buds change

g r e e n   e y e s .

the one for me

he won't be like them

he'll take one look into my eyes

and realize he could never possibly say goodbye

he won't be like the other guys

he'll dive right in

with the ability to actually swim

w e i g h t   l i f t s .

I know now that my words matter

God's built me new

my whole life He's been sculpting me

for far too long I was held back

I'm finally falling into the purpose He's had for me

but I'll be honest it scares me a lot

putting my words out here in the open

for everyone to know

just how far He once was from me

they are all going to see clearly

what I've been through

and that scares me more than anything

it's easy to be vulnerable behind the screen

but to bind my words to a spine

it's going to put me to the test

printing them in a book like this

it's a weight off my chest

it terrifies my heart

I'll be honest

writing this whole thing

has already torn me apart

it's torn me into pieces

through each season

I know there was a reason

I know the aches didn't go to waste

there's been so much healing in this place

o c e a n   e y e s .

now when I cry

it's because of the work

that God has done in my heart

He's changed me from the inside out

it's a feeling I'm crazy about

how to lead her.

follow Jesus,
the end.

note to heart.

be with someone

who compliments your calling

not someone who confuses you about it

things you should do more of.

laugh.

create.

pray.

travel.

speak.

read.

play.

breathe.

write.

kiss.

listen.

dream.

how will i know.

how will I know?
I think it's when he speaks straight to my soul
to who I really am because of Whose I am
I think it's when we talk and my spirit feels alive
I'll feel like the real me can come out from the inside
I think it's when we connect on a level that seems
supernatural, like it's just too good to be true
I think it's when I realize what God already knew
I think it's when he brings peace instead of pain
I think it's when the sweet sound of his voice
tells my heart that I'll forever be his choice
I think it's when I can breathe easy because
I know I'm finally home
home to be free
to fully be me
to be fully known
to realize that I'll never spend another night alone

but most of all, I think it's when

he starts to bring out the God colors in my heart

he'll be the artist with the brush,

and I'll be the writer with the pen

and in that moment we'll ask each other,

'my love, where on this earth have you been?'

I think that's how I will know.

r e c o v e r y   m o d e .

the doctor called today

he had something new to say

he told me that I have a break in the lead

the one that my heart needs

it's been connected to me for six years

but he tells me I don't need to fear

a break like this can happen over time

and at an age like mine

with all the activity that I do

it was bound to happen, like he already knew

so he's not surprised

and with the same calm in his voice

he tells me I don't have much of a choice

I'll need surgery to place a new lead

but there's a big risk that comes with this

removing the old lead isn't as easy as it seems

the irony in this makes me want to scream

it sounds a lot like us, correct me if I'm wrong

we were connected for so long

we were young and so much time had passed

that eventually all the wear and tear

that you put on my heart

ended up breaking us apart

and while you've been busy putting on a show

I've let God do my healing, resting in recovery mode

I feel it now, eventually I'll reap what I've sowed

and just like this device in my chest

God will replace you with something new, aka His

best

c u r r e n t l y .

dripping in honesty,

soaked in grace

l i f e   w i t h o u t   m e .

I guess I just wonder
was it all worth it?

b u t   r e a l l y .

you deserve more than a double tap on your feed
you deserve a man who can actually lead

m e s s y   h e a r t   k n o t s .

is he willing to climb into your thoughts
and undo all your messy little heart knots?

e v e r y w h e r e .

I'm craving a touch

one that cracks open my soul

to the adventurous life

that I've always wanted to know

p u z z l e   m a k e r .

let God put you two together

He knows you're not playing around

He knows where all the missing pieces can be found

b a c k d o o r   l o v e .

you tell yourself you won't let another one in

you can't, not after where you've been

you're scared

much more than you'd ever admit

but this one will understand

and he'll do something

that no one's ever done before

he'll go through the back door

he'll know that the rest of your heart is too sore

and that's the only way he'll be able to get inside

he'll make you forget that you were trying to hide

n o t h i n g   t o   f e a r .

it's okay to be scared

but don't let the fear of something true

keep it from happening to you

just take your time

it's going to be more than fine

don't you remember

when God gave you all those signs?

He's never in the hurry

so you don't have to be either

a new month is coming soon

one that looks nothing like June

the leaves will change colors

and the world will seem like it's brand new

just breathe

don't leave, don't run, don't hide

if you have to, you can cry

but please know that He's working here

this time you have everything to gain

and nothing to fear

n e w s f l a s h .

I get it

you've been hurt before

in a way that makes it difficult to stay

only because the one before

made it hard to breathe

he was always the one to leave

so you're scared to try again

I get it and Jesus does too

but newsflash pretty girl

He's got someone tailor made just for you

y o u r   w i l d   m e s s .

I want to be held

but I want to run free

I need you to be unafraid of loving the wild in me

don't forget.

your mess won't ever disqualify you from God's best

full circle.

everyone keeps asking me how I'm feeling

and I tell them that I'm filled with peace

but I'm beginning to lose sleep at night

I'm trying not to let my heart put up a fight

because I knew that this had to happen

for the last year God has healed my broken heart

and now this surgery is just the cherry on top of it all

to the healing process that started last Fall

it's full circle now

for so long I felt like I was the one losing

but this process is about to be completed

and finally, I no longer feel like I'm the one defeated

i f   i t   f l o w s .

when God's behind it, it's easy

it's like your soul will just know

you can rest easy because peace is there to stay

there's no force to push against

because it's just how it was always suppose to be

if you have to force it, let it go

if it flows, then you know.

i   n e e d   s o m e o n e .

to pray with me

to lay with me

to stay with me

o n   t h e   o t h e r   s i d e .

did you hear about my heart?

yes, this time - I'm talking about you

I'd bet my life on it - watch, you won't come through

but that's nothing new

trust me, just because we've been apart

it doesn't mean I don't think about how it would be

if you were there at the hospital with me

I know you still care about me

how could you not after all those years?

but what does it matter

you're too afraid to face your fears

this hurts so much

more than you'll ever know

but I guess maybe when these doctors open me up

I can finally let you go

and then God can do a miracle on the other side

for now, all He needs me to do is abide

s w e e t   h e a r t .

I tell everyone not to worry about me

because I just know that I'll be more than okay

Jesus will be there that day

and plus, I still have this world to see

with my future husband who deserves this

sweet heart that God's fixing inside of me

l e t ' s   m a k e   a   d e a l .

I'll bring you My best,

if you keep Me first.

- God to me, maybe to you too

s o m e t h i n g   d i f f e r e n t .

it won't be like anything that you were use to

that's the thing about letting God heal your heart

He gets you wanting something new in the process

something different

something that looks nothing like before

something impossible to ignore

something that makes you realize from the start

that you just know is right

because it's so easy

o p e n   a t   t h e   s e a m s .

I have to remind myself every day

that I've come such a long way

I'm not nearly as sad as I use to be

but then I get a text

it's not from you, that's nothing new

but from the one who raised you

to be everything that you aren't right now

I was at show when it came through

this time – it was an artist that I knew

and as he sings about heartbreak

my own heart starts to ache

and when I read the text

it felt like the place in my heart where we use to be

opened up at the seams, I could barely breathe

like it was prepping me for this surgery

and as I made on my way home that night

of course the road led me past where you live

the tears well up in my eyes as I drive by

I pray that your sober

because if I'm honest, all I want to do is come over

I want to turn left and go through the gate

for a second, I hit my brakes

but my heart presses on, feeling like it's too late

so I go home and lie on my floor

like too many times before

I barely have the strength anymore

with tears streaming down my face

I ask God once again to come into this place

w i s h f u l   t h i n k i n g .

I wish you were sober long enough to see

just how much you mean to Jesus and me

i n   t h e   t i d e .

it's so much harder than everyone thinks
it's like standing on the shore
watching your favorite ship sink
I want to save you but I know that I can't
because you're out there drowning in your fear
and I'm over here, sensing a miracle is near
but I can't get it if I leave this place with Him
because I know I'll get caught in the tide of your sin
and I can't do that to me
and I can't do that to you
I guess I'll just keep praying you come home soon

miracle ready.

I get it now

as hard as this will be for me

there are just some things that I don't get to see

God's called me to go into this surgery on my own

but I'm okay because I know I won't really be alone

and this will make me full grown

into the woman He needs me to be

so I'm ready for the miracle that He's promised me

n o   w o n d e r .

the sun is up and I'm laying here in this hospital room

I get to go home soon

my new scar starts aching at the site of the incision

the doctors knew it was an easy decision

to go through the same one as they did before

no wonder it's more than just sore

it was just like opening us back up

and when they did, it looked so messy inside

no wonder all you could do was hide

you've always been so good at pushing me to the side

and you still have nothing to say

let's be real, if I meant anything to you

you really would have been there that day

it wouldn't have mattered how much time had passed

if you still loved me, you would've been there and fast

I think that's what makes me so sick

that if the roles were switched and you were me

I would have given up the world

just to be there with you

g o l d e n   a c h e s .

I get home and lay in bed

it's no surprise, not a word has been said

all I can do is cry

my entire body fills with pain when I move it

even an inch to the side

I look at my new scar

the one that covers up the old

and I think to myself

how could someone possibly see the gold?

I know God's doing something new

I know He's making me more like Him

but right now, if I'm honest

I wonder if I'll ever feel pretty again

I mean who could really love a girl like me

with all these bruises and this scar for everyone to see?

my throat is in pain

my stomach is in knots

my heart is aching

it feels like it's breaking

s h o w i n g   u p .

I get it, you thought he'd come through

you thought even after everything

he would have showed up

given everything he knew

but he didn't

and it's breaking your heart all over again

don't let his choice to not show up

make you think that you're not worthy of love

you are worthy of a love that shows up

day in and day out

no matter what

no matter who

no matter where

your heart deserves a love that forever shows up

don't ever forget that

b e d   r e s t   t h o u g h t s .

this recovery is harder than it seems

the pain inside my heart

the ache in stomach

the bruises on my arms

the scar on my chest

it all hurts so much, but it's nothing compared

to how it feels not hearing from you

after everything we've been through

I really thought you'd have something to say

but I know you're still so lost

I think back to the last time

I heard your voice

remember back in the new year?

I was overseas so we talked on the phone

it was a conversation I couldn't help but fear

I still remember it loud and clear

you said you'd stop smoking

you said you needed to be better

so I believed you for a minute

and kept writing you letters

but then I got home

yet you didn't want to see me

you said it'd take time to make the change

9 months later and you're still the same

you've hurt me so much

you don't even know

what I would still give for you to pick up the phone

I know the guy that I fell in love with

is still in there somewhere

your friends and family know it too

but the only problem is

that you have to choose

for yourself to believe it too

#askingforafriend
part II

is it possible to give it some distance

and hope that the resistance

pushes hard enough to cause a change?

m e r c y .

I see photos of you these days

and it makes my heart break

seeing you literally covered up by all the haze

God has so much more in store

and I know that you know it too

remember when He first came through for you?

that day in the back of the cop car

you've never been too far

and you aren't now, no matter where you've been

I hope you know that I'm rooting for you

but it's a whisper in my heart because

right now if we spoke the tears would come quick

and I know it'd make my heart sick

you have so much potential and I know it's essential

that you go through this on your own

so you can break just like I did

and let Jesus lead you back home

b e t t e r   t h a n .

His blessings are better than I dreamed

His ways are sweeter than I hoped

His plans are greater than I knew

He's healed me in a way that only He could do

and I pray as you've read through these words

that there has been some sort of healing for you too

t i l l   n e x t   s e a s o n .

now you ask, what will I write next?

and how could I end it like this,

wanting the best for him, after all he did?

well if I'm honest, it's all my heart has ever wanted

some may say that I'm far too sweet but

when the doctors opened me up that day it was like

all the extra love in my heart for him spilled out

like a broken spout

and I was bleeding from the inside out

and I finally was able to let it go

in a way that was healing for my heart

that I didn't even know

it allowed me to see that life is way too short

to hold onto the hurt that he caused

and even if he lost himself back then

my heart won't ever truly give up

on wanting him to find his true self again

because I found out who I am

through this whole thing

and it's the sweetest thing that I know

which is what I needed all along

to serve my purpose, for His name, through my pain

I've never felt more loved by the Lord

sure I don't know what's ahead

but I know that I needed to break on my own

in every sense of the word

to face my own sin

so I could become full grown

and now that I am

I can see that this whole thing

was never really about me

it was about His glory, through my story

so as far as what's next

well He's the one with the pen

and I guess as I rest and recover

I'll write about the things that I start to discover

and I'll tell you all about it next season

once He shows me the reasons

to be continued...

T H A N K   Y O U

Mom.

For being there when no one else was.
For wiping away my tears when they seemed never
ending. For helping me see the light when the
darkness came. For loving me fiercely,
unconditionally, and relentlessly.
My love for love stems from the love
that your heart has always shown mine.

Dad.

For always choosing me. For loving me despite my
mistakes. For giving me strength when I lost mine.
For sticking by me when it hurt the most. For
supporting me through each and every valley I've
ever had to walk through.

I love you both, more than words could ever say.
A thank you will never be able to cover just how grateful I am
for your love. Forever you'll be my two favorite people.

Made in the USA
Lexington, KY
19 October 2017